Hedley

by Jennifer Sutoski

CAPSTONE PRESS
a capstone imprint

Pebble Plus is published by Capstone Press,
1710 Roe Crest Drive, North Mankato, Minnesota 56003
www.capstonepub.com

Library of Congress Cataloging-in-Publication Data
Cataloging-in-publication information is on file with the Library of Congress.

ISBN 978–1-4914-7837-0 (library binding : alk. paper)
ISBN 978–1-4914-7845-5 (pbk. : alk. paper)
ISBN 978–1-4914-7860-8 (eBook PDF)

Developed and Produced by Discovery Books Limited
Paul Humphrey: project manager
Sabrina Crewe: editor
Ian Winton: designer

Photo Credits
Michael Hurcomb/Corbis: cover, 21; Mark Horton/Corbis: title page, 15; Igor Vidyashev/ZUMA Press/Corbis: 5; Elsa/Getty Images: 7; Ruigsantos/Shutterstock: 9 (top); Reuters/Steve Marcus/Corbis: 9 (bottom); Mike Cassese/Reuters/Corbis: 11; Richard Heathcote/Getty Images: 13; Courtesy of Free the Children: 17, 19 (both).

Note to Parents and Teachers
The Canadian Biographies set supports national curriculum standards for social studies related to people and culture. This book describes and illustrates Hedley. The images support early readers in understanding text. The repetition of words and phrases helps early readers learn new words. This book also introduces early readers to subject-specific vocabulary words, which are defined in the Glossary section. Early readers may need assistance to read some words and to use the Table of Contents, Glossary, Read More, Internet Sites, and Index sections of the book.

Printed in China through World Print Ltd in 2015
007326WPF15

Table of Contents

A New Band

Hedley is a famous Canadian music group. Jacob (Jake) Hoggard is the lead singer. He plays piano and guitar, too. Dave Rosin plays the guitar. Tommy Mac plays bass guitar, and Chris Crippin is the drummer.

From left to right: Chris, Dave, Jake, and Tommy

In 2004, Jake competed on *Canadian Idol*. He was very popular and came third. After the show, Jake asked Dave, Tommy, and Chris to join his band.

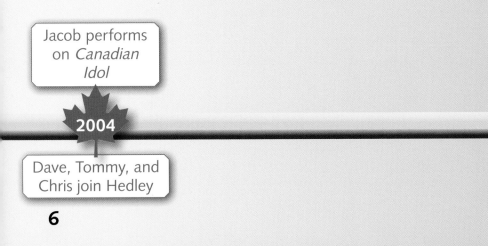

Jacob performs on *Canadian Idol*

2004

Dave, Tommy, and Chris join Hedley

Jake (in red shirt) sings the National Anthem with other *Canadian Idol* finalists.

Number One

Hedley made an agreement with
Capitol Records. Capitol would make
and sell Hedley's singles and albums.
Hedley's first album was just called
Hedley, after the band. The song
"On My Own" went to number one!

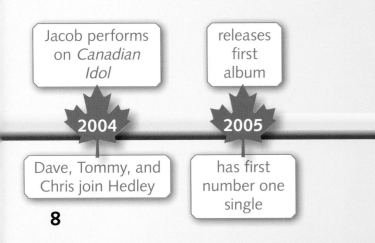

Jacob performs on *Canadian Idol*

releases first album

2004

2005

Dave, Tommy, and Chris join Hedley

has first number one single

The Capitol Records Tower is a famous building in the United States.

Hedley performed in the United States in 2006.

Hedley was famous. The band made more albums and went on tour. Hedley performed at concerts all around Canada. The group's fans loved the band and the music.

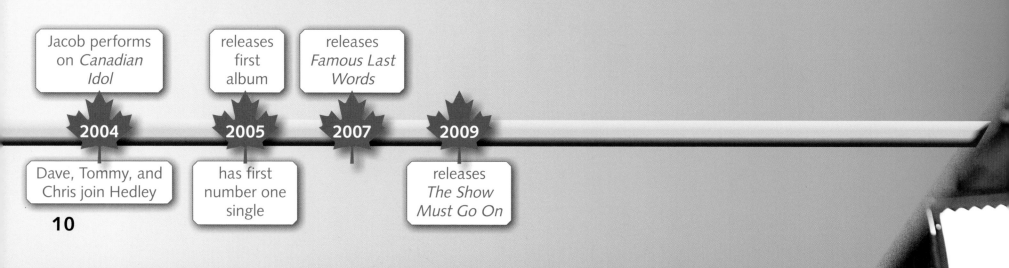

Jacob performs on *Canadian Idol*

releases first album

releases *Famous Last Words*

2004

2005

2007

2009

Dave, Tommy, and Chris join Hedley

has first number one single

releases *The Show Must Go On*

Performing for fans in 2008

By 2010, Hedley was among Canada's favourite bands. The band won awards and topped the charts. Hedley even played at the Olympic Games in Vancouver.

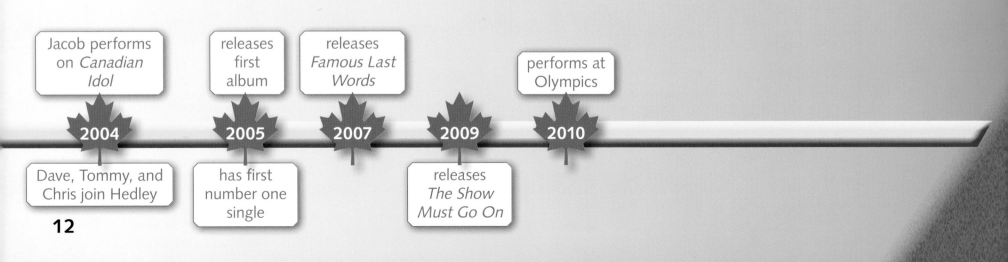

Jacob performs on *Canadian Idol*

releases first album

releases *Famous Last Words*

performs at Olympics

2004 **2005** **2007** **2009** **2010**

Dave, Tommy, and Chris join Hedley

has first number one single

releases *The Show Must Go On*

On stage at the Olympic Games in 2010

Hedley made their fourth album, *Storms*, in 2011. In 2012, Hedley won the Juno Award for pop album of the year. The Juno Awards are Canada's biggest music awards.

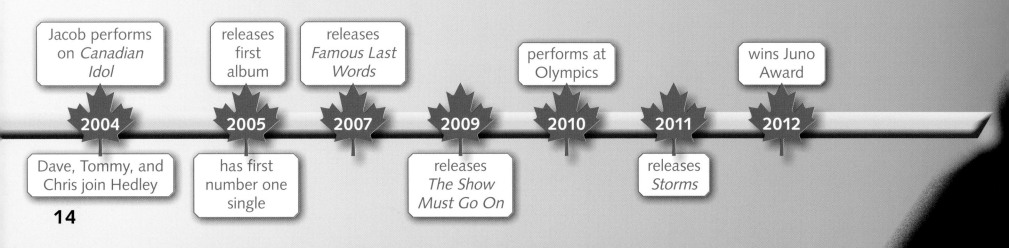

Jacob performs on *Canadian Idol*

releases first album

releases *Famous Last Words*

performs at Olympics

wins Juno Award

2004   **2005**   **2007**   **2009**   **2010**   **2011**   **2012**

Dave, Tommy, and Chris join Hedley

has first number one single

releases *The Show Must Go On*

releases *Storms*

Accepting the Juno Award in 2012

Doing Good

Chris, Dave, Jake, and Tommy work with two charities, Free the Children and Me to We. Free the Children helps children around the world. Me to We shows young Canadians how they can help, too.

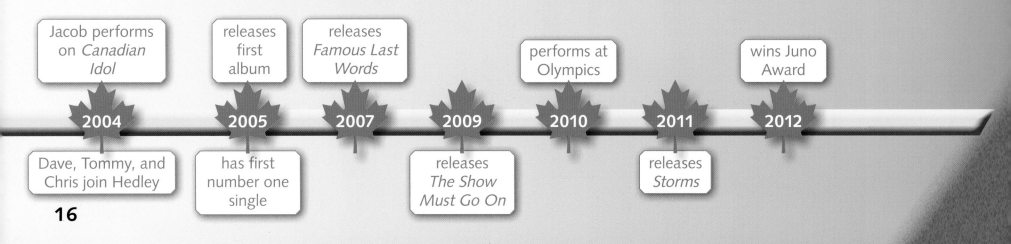

Jacob performs on *Canadian Idol*

2004

Dave, Tommy, and Chris join Hedley

releases first album

2005

has first number one single

releases *Famous Last Words*

2007

2009

releases *The Show Must Go On*

performs at Olympics

2010

2011

releases *Storms*

wins Juno Award

2012

Hedley in India with Free the Children founder Craig Kielburger (back row, second from left)

Hedley went to Kenya and to India to help. Then, in 2014, the band went to Ecuador to build a school. Hedley's fans gave more than $10,000 to help with the project.

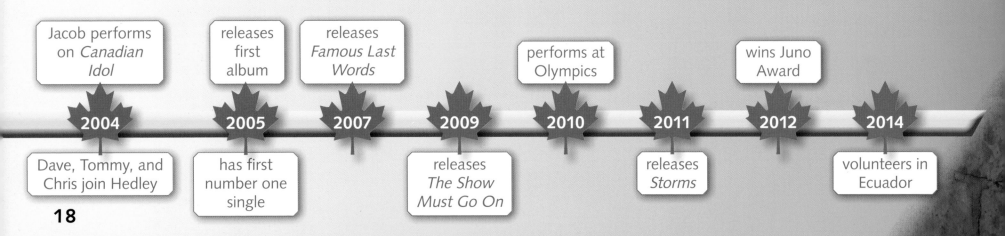

Jacob performs on *Canadian Idol*

releases first album

releases *Famous Last Words*

performs at Olympics

wins Juno Award

2004 **2005** **2007** **2009** **2010** **2011** **2012** **2014**

Dave, Tommy, and Chris join Hedley

has first number one single

releases *The Show Must Go On*

releases *Storms*

volunteers in Ecuador

Members of Hedley in Kenya with Me to We

Doing Better

Hedley has many awards and lots of fans. The band plans to do more in the future. In 2014, Jacob Hoggard said, "We shoot to do everything that we do a little bit better each time."

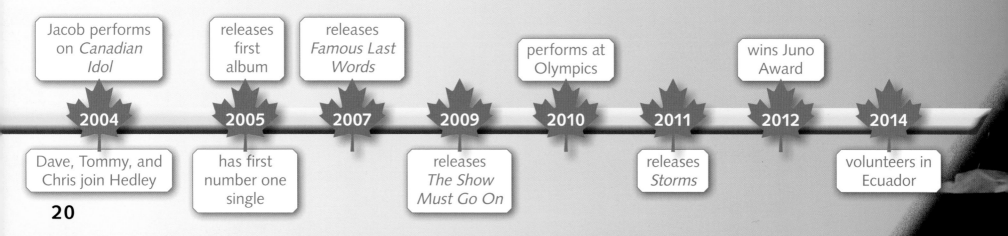

Jacob performs on *Canadian Idol*

releases first album

releases *Famous Last Words*

performs at Olympics

wins Juno Award

2004   **2005**   **2007**   **2009**   **2010**   **2011**   **2012**   **2014**

Dave, Tommy, and Chris join Hedley

has first number one single

releases *The Show Must Go On*

releases *Storms*

volunteers in Ecuador

Hedley on stage in 2014

Glossary

album—a set of songs under one title

award—something people get for winning or doing well

band—a group of musicians

bass guitar—an electric guitar with a deep sound

charts—a table showing which songs and bands are selling the most

compete—to enter a contest against other people

fan—a person who admires or follows a performer

lead singer—the singer who does most of the singing

popular—liked by a lot of people

single—one song released by itself

tour—a journey made with stops for performing

Read More

Hedley. *http://www.hedleyonline.com.* Find out more about Hedley on their website.

Kielburger, Craig. *Lessons from a Street Kid.* Toronto, ON: Me to We Books, 2011.

Kielburger, Marc. *Everyone's Birthday.* Toronto, ON: Me to We Books, 2012.

Internet Sites

FactHound offers a safe, fun way to find Internet sites related to this book. All of the sites on FactHound have been researched by our staff.

Here's all you do:

Visit *www.facthound.com*

Type in this code: 9781491478370

Check out projects, games and lots more at
www.capstonekids.com

Index

Word Count: 283
Grade: 1
Early-Intervention Level: 17